Printed in Great Britain
by Amazon

35316974R00057